Emperor Penguins
Up Close

Carmen Bredeson

E Enslow Elementary

CONTENTS

WORDS TO KNOW

Antarctica (ant ARK tih kuh)—The ice-covered land around the South Pole.

beak—The hard, pointed part of a bird's mouth.

krill—Small, shrimplike animals that penguins eat.

waddle (WAH dul)—To walk by leaning from side to side.

Parts of an Emperor Penguin

head

beak

wing

chick

belly flap

tail

claws

EMPEROR PENGUIN

Emperor penguins are the biggest penguins in the world. They grow to be almost four feet tall.

Emperor penguins live in
Antarctica, the coldest place
on Earth.

PENGUIN WINGS

Penguins are birds, but they cannot fly. Their wings are too short. Their bodies are too heavy.

Emperor penguins swim very fast in the sea. Their wings flap, flap, flap. The more the wings flap, the faster the penguin swims.

PENGUIN FEATHERS

UP CLOSE

Shiny feathers and a layer of fat keep penguins warm. Black feathers grow on the back and head. White feathers cover the belly.

Every year, old feathers fall out. New feathers grow in.

LEAPING PENGUINS

Emperor penguins live mostly in the sea. Once a year they leap onto land. It is time to lay their eggs.

The penguins walk and walk across the ice. It looks like a penguin parade.

10

PENGUIN FEET

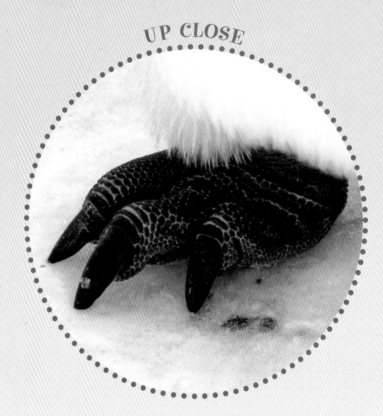

Walking is not something penguins do very well. They waddle from side to side. Sharp claws on their webbed feet grip the ice.

Sometimes the birds flop onto their bellies and slide. Sliding is easier than walking.

PENGUIN EGG

egg

Each mother penguin lays one egg. Father scoops the egg onto his feet. The egg fits under a flap of his belly skin. Then mother waddles and slides back to the sea. Father keeps the egg on his feet for TWO MONTHS!

Father penguins stand very close together. They keep
each other warm while they keep their eggs warm!

PENGUIN CHICK

UP CLOSE

chick on
father's
feet

One day there is a tap, tap, tap from the egg.
A little chick comes out. Father makes a kind of
milk in his throat. He feeds his hungry chick.
The chick stays warm on its father's feet. The
baby penguin grows and grows.

PENGUIN BEAK

Mother penguin comes back to feed her new chick. Father finally gets to go to the sea. He has not eaten for over three months.

Watch out shrimp, fish, and krill! Here comes the penguin's long black and orange beak. *Gulp*.

krill ▶

PENGUIN FAMILY

Soon father penguin is full. He goes back to his family on land. Both parents feed their peeping chick. The little penguin grows and grows. When it is five months old, it will go to sea for the first time.

These chicks are standing at the edge of the water.
It is time to jump into the sea.

LIFE CYCLE

Mother lays egg.
Father keeps egg on his feet.

Chick hatches.
Father keeps
chick on his feet.

Adult has
babies when
it is five
years old.

Five-month-
old penguin
goes to sea.

22

LEARN MORE

BOOKS

Butterfield, Moira. *Animals in Cold Places*. Austin, Tex.: Raintree Steck-Vaughn, 2000.

Chester, Jonathan. *The Nature of Penguins*. Berkeley, Calif.: Celestial Arts, 2001.

Jenkins, Martin. *The Emperor's Egg*. Cambridge, Mass.: Candlewick Press, 1999.

WEB SITES

National Geographic for Kids

<http://kids.nationalgeographic.com/>

Click on "Animals." Then click on "Browse all creatures." Then choose "Emperor Penguins."

Wildlife of Antarctica

<http://www.antarcticconnection.com/antarctic/wildlife/penguins/emperor.shtml>

INDEX

Series Literacy Consultant:
Allan A. De Fina, Ph.D.
Past President of the New Jersey Reading Association
Professor, Department of Literacy Education
New Jersey City University
Jersey City, New Jersey

Science Consultant:
Paul L. Sieswerda
Aquarium Curator
New York Aquarium
Brooklyn, New York

Note to Parents and Teachers: The **Zoom In on Animals!** series supports the National Science Education Standards for K–4 science. The Words to Know section introduces subject-specific vocabulary words, including pronunciation and definitions. Early readers may need help with these new words.

For Andrew and Charlie, our wonderful grandsons

Enslow Elementary, an imprint of Enslow Publishers, Inc.

Enslow Elementary® is a registered trademark of Enslow Publishers, Inc.

Copyright © 2006 by Carmen Bredeson

Library of Congress Cataloging-in-Publication Data

Bredeson, Carmen.
  Emperor penguins up close / Carmen Bredeson.
     p. cm. — (Zoom in on animals!)
  Includes index.
  ISBN-10: 0-7660-2497-0 (hardcover)
  1. Emperor penguin—Juvenile literature. I. Title.
  II. Series.
  QL696.S473B73 2006
  598.47—dc22
                                        2005003331

ISBN-13: 978-0-7660-2497-7

Printed in the United States of America

10 9 8 7 6 5 4 3 2

To Our Readers: We have done our best to make sure all Internet Addresses in this book were active and appropriate when we went to press. However, the author and the publisher have no control over and assume no liability for the material available on those Internet sites or on other Web sites they may link to. Any comments or suggestions can be sent by e-mail to comments@enslow.com or to the address on the back cover.

Photo Credits: ©1999, Artville, LLC, p. 5 (inset); Bill Curtsinger / National Geographic Image Collection, pp. 8, 18; © Corel Corporation, p. 22 (chick on feet); © Daniel A. Bedell / Animals Animals, pp. 4–5, 6, 10; © Frank Awbrey / Visuals Unlimited, p. 19; © 2005 Frans Lanting / www. lanting.com, pp. 1, 3, 12, 13, 16, 20, 22 (egg, chick, adults); © Gerald L. Kooyman /Animals Animals, p. 21; © Gerald & Buff Corsi / Visuals Unlimited, p. 19; © Graham Robertson / ardea.com, p. 11, 14, 15; © 2005 Norbert Wu / www.norbertwu.com, pp. 7, 9; © 1999 PhotoDisc, Inc., p. 19 (background); © Phyllis Greenberg / Animals Animals, p. 17.

Cover Photos: © 2005 Frans Lanting / www.lanting.com (large image and claw); Bill Curtsinger / National Geographic Image Collection (beak); © Daniel A. Bedell / Animals Animals (wings).

Enslow Elementary
an imprint of
Enslow Publishers, Inc.
40 Industrial Road
Box 398
Berkeley Heights, NJ 07922
USA
http://www.enslow.com